Good Morning Holy Spirit

50 DAYS OF PRAYER AND DEVOTION

Dr. Troye Thigpen

Acknowledgements
Graphic Design
Front and Back Cover

Designed by: Dr. Troye Thigpen - Vision and Design Eva@Miz_Design - Mechanics Front Cover:

Sunrise
https://www.bing.com/images/search?view=detailV2&ccid=doI5TJrS&id=B26CDDEE544EDDA3F1DF2170E24F0EC52EB8094A&thid=OIP.doI5TJrSRJtK291dy69vAEsCh&q=sun+rise&simid=607993261508526463&selectedIndex=16&ajaxhist=0

Silhouette of woman praising God at Sunrise
https://www.bing.com/images/search?view=detailV2&ccid=9FaJ5teo&id=44CDBA309B241BBC7C8CCF7F895E198CAC04C206&thid=OIP.9FaJ5teogqfjUWaA8va-YQEsCp&q=silhouette+of+woman+praising+god&simid=608031808861507273&selectedIndex=101&ajaxhist=0

Man Praising God
https://www.bing.com/images/search?view=detailV2&ccid=5JRVH6ft&id=707D8838B6BA5602EF078CDF9EEFCD9F1E48F975&thid=OIP.5JRVH6ftBs3iGnhaj1vVQEMEs&q=man+worshiping+God&simid=608012726330655382&selectedIndex=188&ajaxhist=0

Back Cover:

Dr. Troye in Worship and Praise to God
Living Motivated
Photography Dr. Walter
Sims
www.livingmotivatedphotography.com

Dedication

This book Good Morning Holy Spirit is dedicated
to God the Father and His Holy Spirit that
inspired this splendid work.
Without His Wisdom, Knowledge, and
Understanding, this book would not be possible.

I also would like to dedicate this book to my
wonderful family. My husband Reggy and our
beautiful children Chloe Jae, and Reggy II. My
precious grandparents Fred and Geneva White
Martin (She was my praying grandmother. I saw her
prayers and faith in action.) My Aunts and Uncles,
Jeanette and Johnny Moss, Sr; Roslyn and Clarence
Hatcher, and Mable Reddick. Along with my cousins
and extended family.

I could not move forward without mentioning my
wonderful Mother and Father in love, Dorothy, and
Lawrence Thigpen. All I can say is God knew what I
needed, and He provided.
You two are God's gift to our family and me. My
wonderful Sister and brother in Love, Raquelle
and Bruce Hunter.

My first "Baby Boy," my brother, Coren Wilson and our loving parents, Ronald and Clementine Wilson. I know that they are looking down from their Heavenly Home proud of their children and grandchildren. We shall continue to make them proud.

Our precious friends who encourage and support us at The Prayer Tent International with your testimonies of God's miraculous power.

Contents

Foreword

50 DAYS OF PRAYER...A CATALYST FOR YOUR
WALK IN CHRIST

I have been knowing Troye for nearly 20 years, and
one thing that is pronounced about her life is her
passion for the presence of God, her passion for
prayer, and her passion for people. This is captured
in every devotional that she has provided to be a
blessing to all who not only read it but will take a
few minutes daily to make it a part of their lives.
Here is why "50 Days of Prayer" will bless you:

1. It is a tool that will nurture your intimacy
    with God, and it is centered in truth because
    this tool has its basis in the word of God.

2. It is a prayer map that suggests a strategy
    for interaction with The Holy Spirit that will
    enhance your prayer and devotional life.

3. It will foster healthy internal dialogue to
    support you in applying what you receive
    in your daily life.

4. Your spirit will be fed: thus, bringing
    strength, encouragement, and wisdom to

support you in dealing with the multiple battles that we face every day.

Enjoy this devotional; it is a gift from God through Troye to be a blessing to you!

Apostle Roger C. Kelly, Sr., CLU, ChFC
Eaglevision Consulting Group
Spiritual and Financial Consultant
Author: The E-Model: Prospering Beyond the Economic Storm

Preface

Prepare your heart for transformation over the next
50-days. Troye Thigpen, following the leading by
Holy Spirit, has charted a path of surrender, prayer,
meditation, and worship that will lead you into a
more intimate relationship with Holy Spirit. This
book is a series of interactive prayers/meditations
that cause you to explore your relationship with
Holy Spirit. As you move through progressive
questions, you will be challenged to open your
heart to Holy Spirit and allow Him to minister to
the most secret parts of your heart. You will find
that you will be more sensitive to His leading and
find you're sharing with others to more precise and
compassionate.

Upon completion of this book, you will want to share
it with everyone that you care about because you will
want them to experience Holy Spirit as you have. I
encourage you not to wait until the end but to invite a
friend or a small group to take this journey with you.
However, you choose to study, if it is with friends or
alone, you will be blessed.

Troye is a dedicated prayer warrior who prays
intensively at least two times per day: 3 am & 3 pm.
She is worshiping and warring while you are busy
with the cares of your life. Join her on this path of

transformational worship and warring with Holy Spirit and your life will be changed forever!

Dr. Dominique Baptiste, President
Spirit & Truth Christian University

Introduction

When Moses was called and chosen by God, there was a great encounter, as he stood at the burning bush. The bush burned with the fire and presence of God, yet, the bush remained. God spoke to Moses from that Holy place; He told him that He had heard the cries and the moans of His people. So, He decided to come down. When God came down, He saw the oppression and suppression of His people, at the hands of the taskmasters and decided to deliver them from Egyptian control. He called Moses by name and told him that He wanted him to go and talk to Pharaoh and bring them out of Egypt. Moses made excuses as to why he could not fulfill his calling. Moses, seeing God's displeasure with his response, consented to His plan with the help of his brother Aaron. Eventually, they passed over The Red Sea with celebration and praise. Crossing over The Red Sea was God's great Salvation plan. It took those 50 days to pass through the Red Sea, travel through the wilderness, consecrate themselves, and stand at the foot of the mountain of God, Mt. Sinai, where God spoke to them. This journey is known as the first Pentecost. The number fifty means Pentecost.

God wanted the Israelites to be His people, and He wanted to be their God. They went from having judges to Kings. God did not want them to have kings, but He granted their wishes. The Israelites continued in their disobedience. They could not keep the laws of God, because of their sin.

The prophets of the Old Testament prophesied of the coming of Jesus. A Savior that would come and save us from our sins, heal the brokenhearted, bring sight to the blind, and set the captive free.

Jesus did come. He was born of a virgin woman, grew in wisdom and stature and had favor with God and men. He began His ministry after He was baptized by John the Baptist and endowed with the Holy Spirit of God. The Holy Spirit remained with Jesus until He died on the cross. It was the Holy Spirit of God that assisted Jesus with His ministry. He led Jesus into the wilderness for 40 days and nights, where Jesus was tempted, tested, and tried, yet He never sinned. The Holy Spirit was with Jesus when He called the 12 Disciples, healed "All" sickness and disease, preached the Good News, cast out demons, and raised the dead.

After Jesus died on the cross, He returned and visited some of the 12 Disciples and followers for 40 days. Before He ascended to Heaven to take His seat at the right hand of His Father, He instructed them to go and stay in Jerusalem. Jesus told them to stay there and wait for "The Promise" of the Father- the Baptism of the Holy Spirit of God. The Bible says that they went to the Upper Room and devoted themselves to prayer, as a unified body. On the 50th day, the "Day of Pentecost," they were altogether praying, and the Holy Spirit of God came and filled the whole house. They were all saved and filled with the "Gift of the Promise."

The Holy Spirit of God came in and filled their hearts, and they became the temple of the Holy Spirit of God. God's Spirit came to live and dwell inside of them, to lead them and guide them into all truth. To this day, the same thing happens to any and every individual who asks Jesus to come into their hearts.

In the first Pentecost, the Israelites were set free From oppression, suppression, and depression. The yoke of bondage and slavery were removed, but their minds were not renewed and free because of the years of slavery. They did not have the Spirit of God living and dwelling inside of them, only the law. The Spirit of God would come upon them to do His will.

In the second Pentecost, the Disciples that were in the Upper Room were transformed, renewed with Jesus' cleansing fire, and baptized by the Holy Spirit of God. The prophecies of the Old Testament Prophets were fulfilled. John the Baptist foretold that Jesus would baptize with the Holy Spirit and with fire. I thank God that He did.

There have been times when I have been in prayer, and I heard the Spirit of God speak to me, and exactly 50 days later, they have come to fruition. So, when I heard the Spirit of God say Good Morning Holy Spirit: 50 Days of Prayer and Devotion, it was not a mystery to me. I had already begun to write and share these prayers with many, but God was provoking me to reach more people for His kingdom.

You see, it was from a place of pain that I began to write these prayers. I know the voice of God. I know when He speaks to me. There is a nudging in my Spirit that will not lift until the assignment is complete. It was during this time that I had to stand alone. Just like Moses. Have you ever had that feeling? As painful as it was at that time, I had to be obedient to God and do and say what He required of me, although those closest to me did not understand. It was the Holy Spirit of God that gave me great comfort through the pen of these 50 prayers and many others. It was the Holy Spirit of God who spoke to my Spirit and told me what to write and how to write it. It was His wisdom, knowledge, and understanding that guided me along the way. It was the prayers from the Great Intercessor, Jesus that brought healing to my soul as I began to write and share these prayers with others.

o   I pray that as you read, Good Morning Holy Spirit: 50 Days of Prayer and Devotion, you will be transformed, renewed, restored, and set free from anything that will stop the flow of the Spirit of God moving and flowing in your life

o   I pray that your relationship with our loving Father and His Son, Jesus Christ, will be forever changed.

o   I pray that as you read each prayer daily and you meditate on each Scripture, the Holy Spirit of God will speak to you as He did to me in my time of fellowship and devotion with Him.

o   I pray that He heals every broken place, mind, body, and soul.

o   I pray that He will help you take every
thought captive that does not line up with the Word
of God for your life and your family's life.

o   I pray that the Holy Spirit will bring you
immense joy

o   I pray that He will inform you, instruct you,
and grant you much favor as you grow in the
wisdom and knowledge of God in these 50 days.

o   I pray that you will have a great encounter
like Moses, a resurrection like Jesus, and freedom like
me. Make it a "Pentecostal" experience. Your own
"Personal and Purposeful," experience with God.

There is one thing that I know about God when you
make a commitment, or shall I say an appointment
with Him, consistently. You do not have to worry.
He will be there. He will show up. He is truly
committed to you, and He is committed to prayer. He
created us to have relationship and fellowship with
Him.

OUR PRAYER!

Day 1 - Reveal the Hidden Things

Good Morning Holy Spirit!

Thank You for Your Wisdom, Knowledge, and Power. Reveal to us the hidden things. Things that have been hidden in darkness until its appointed time. For You, God, are surrounded by Your Glorious Light, and where there is light, darkness will no longer be.

Thank You for answers to secrets. Only you have the answers to reveal Your Prophecy, the future things. The plans you have for us to prosper, have a future, and hope.

When we call You, You will come and listen to us as we pray.

OUR PRAYER!

Day 1

Gentle Whispers from Holy Spirit

Today's Scriptures: Daniel 2: 17-23; Jeremiah 29:11-12

Did Holy Spirit speak to you?

What would you add to the prayer to make it personal to you?

Day 2 - Your Unfailing Love

Good Morning Holy Spirit!

Thank You for Your unfailing love. There is no one like you. You are great, and Your Name is full of Power! Among all the wise people of the earth and in all the kingdoms of the world, there is no one like you.

 You, Lord, are the only True God, our everlasting Father.

OUR PRAYER!

Day 2

Gentle Whispers from Holy Spirit

Today's Scriptures: Jeremiah 9:24; 10:6-10

Did Holy Spirit speak to you?

What would you add to the prayer to make it personal to you?

Day 3 - Sweeter Than Honey

Good Morning Holy Spirit!

Thank You for Your Presence and Your Word. How sweet are Your Words to taste! They are sweeter than honey to our mouths. Your Words bring joy, delight, and rejoicing in our hearts.

We are thankful that we are called and protected by Your Name JEHOVAH GOD, LORD of HEAVENS ARMIES.

We give you thanks.

OUR PRAYER!

Day 3

Gentle Whispers from Holy Spirit

Today's Scriptures: Jeremiah 15:16; Psalm 119:103

Did Holy Spirit speak to you?

What would you add to the prayer to make it personal to you?

Day 4 - Chart Our Ways

Good Morning Holy Spirit!

Thank You for Blessing us. Our trust, faith, hope, and confidence are in you. Because we delight in the Law of the Lord and meditate in it day and night, we shall be like trees planted by rivers of water, bringing forth fruit that will never stop producing. We shall prosper in all that we do, for the Lord charts the way of the righteous, and we are the righteousness of God in Christ Jesus.

OUR PRAYER!

Day 4

Gentle Whispers from Holy Spirit

Today's Scriptures: Jeremiah 17:7-8; Psalms 1; 2 Corinthians 5:21

Did Holy Spirit speak to you?

What would you add to the prayer to make it personal to you?

Day 5 - The Place of Rest

Good Morning Holy Spirit!

We worship you at your throne. You are high, eternal, and GLORIOUS!

You truly heal, and you truly save. Our Praise is for you alone. You are our hope and safety in times of trouble.

Keep us in your secret place. The place of rest. In Your shadow and under your wings is where we want to be.

For you are Our God, the Almighty One. We put ALL our trust in you!

OUR PRAYER!

Day 5

Gentle Whispers from Holy Spirit

Today's Scriptures: Jeremiah 17:13-18; Psalms 91:1: 1-2

Did Holy Spirit speak to you?

What would you add to the prayer to make it personal to you?

Day 6 - The Secret Place

Good Morning Holy Spirit!

Thank You for listening when we pray. You always find us in the Secret Place. The place where we pray to you and worship you in Spirit and Truth, wholeheartedly. Your ears are open to the cry of the Righteous, and your eyes roam to and fro.

Thank You for Your delivering and saving power.

Thank You for Your Promises. The good things you have in store for us. Before the world was framed you knew the plans, you had to prosper us. Plans for a great future and hope.

Let others be a witness of Your Goodness towards us.

OUR PRAYER!

Day 6

Gentle Whispers from Holy Spirit

Today's Scriptures: Jeremiah 29:11-13; Psalms 91:1; John 4:23; Psalms 34:15; 1 Peter 3:12; 2 Chronicles 16:9

Did Holy Spirit speak to you?

What would you add to the prayer to make it personal to you?

Day 7 - Your Unfailing and Everlasting Love

Good Morning Holy Spirit!

You draw us with your unfailing and everlasting love. We shall sing with joy, dance merrily, and shout out Your Praise.

Let all join the celebration. For our lives shall be like a watered garden flowing with living water and abundant fruit.

Thank You, Jesus, for your good and perfect gifts. They come from above. Thank You for abundant life.

OUR PRAYER!

Day 7
Gentle Whispers from Holy Spirit

Today's Scriptures: Jeremiah 31: 1-14; John 7:38; James 1:17

Did Holy Spirit speak to you?

What would you add to the prayer to make it personal to you?

Day 8 - A True and Living God

Good Morning Holy Spirit!

We are thankful that old things have passed away, and in you, all things have become new. We are thankful that you remember our sins no more.

We are thankful that we serve a True and Living God. We can repent to you, cry out to you, tell our secrets to You, Pray to You, Praise and Worship You, and give Honor to You.
You look forward to our fellowship with you.

When we come close to You, You come even closer to us. There is no one Like Our God.
For that, we give You Glory and Praise!

OUR PRAYER!

Day 8

Gentle Whispers from Holy Spirit

**Today's Scriptures: 2 Corinthians 5:17;
Psalms 103:12; Jeremiah 10:10; James 4:8**

Did Holy Spirit speak to you?

What would you add to the prayer to make it
personal to you?

Day 9 - We Belong to You

Good Morning Holy Spirit!

The earth is yours and everything that's in it, including us. We belong to you!
Help us to climb Your Mountain and stand in your Holy Place. Help us to maintain clean hands and pure hearts before you.

Thank You for Righteousness and Blessings. You are THE source of all blessings and prosperity, Lord.

We will continue to seek Your Face. You are The King of Glory! Lift Your Everlasting gates and come in. Our lives belong to you!

OUR PRAYER!

Day 9

Gentle Whispers from Holy Spirit

Today's Scriptures: Psalms 24; 25:1

Did Holy Spirit speak to you?

What would you add to the prayer to make it
personal to you?

Day 10 - Speak, Believe, and Trust in the Word of the Lord

Good Morning Holy Spirit!

Thank You for not giving us a Spirit of fear but Power, Love, and a Sound Mind. You said not to be afraid of other faces or what they must say. Do not be dismayed (broken, afraid, discouraged, terrified, or beaten down by them). But speak, believe, and trust in The Word of the Lord. You have set land, things, places, etc. before us to possess.

You said you would go before us, go with us, never fail us, and never forsake us. We are strong and courageous because of you.

We shall Arise, go up, and take possession of what you have given us before the foundation of the world.

We will not back down, but we will stand still and watch the Lord fight our battle.

OUR PRAYER!

Day 10

Gentle Whispers from Holy Spirit

Today's Scriptures: 2nd Timothy 1:7; Ezekiel 2:6; Deuteronomy 1:21; 31:8; Joshua 1:9; 8:1; 2 Chronicles 20:17

Did Holy Spirit speak to you?

What would you add to the prayer to make it personal to you?

Day 11 - Run with it, Work on it, Stay with it

Good Morning Holy Spirit!

Thank You for helping us take hold of the possessions that Christ Jesus has already perfected for us.

Thank You for helping us to stay focused on the goals that lie ahead. The finish line.

Never looking to the past, we press on. Although there may be things that we thought should have or could have happened differently in our lives, we press on.

Help us, Lord, to stay focused on the wisdom, knowledge, and understanding gained from the past to finish the vision that has been written on tablets and set before us. We will run with it, work on it, stay with it.

The Revelation awaits an appointed time, but in the end, it SHALL SPEAK, and come to pass.

OUR PRAYER!

Day 11

Gentle Whispers from Holy Spirit

**Today's Scriptures: Philippians 3:11-14;
Habakkuk 2: 2-3**

Did Holy Spirit speak to you?

What would you add to the prayer to make it
personal to you?

Day 12 - Rock, Strength, Shield, and Deliverer

Good Morning Holy Spirit!

You are our Rock, Strength, Shield, and Deliverer.

Let the words of our mouths and the meditation of our hearts, our minds, and our souls, be acceptable in your sight for you are our Strength and our Redeemer.

There is no other God as Holy as You. There is none beside Thee neither is there any Rock like our God, No one stronger, mightier, or more powerful than our God, and No better place to hide than in the cleft of the rock.

Lord, let Your Glorious Presence pass by us and through us today. Reveal yourself to us in a new way today.

OUR PRAYER!

Day 12

Gentle Whispers from Holy Spirit

Today's Scriptures: Psalm 16:2; 1 Samuel 2:2; Psalms19:14; Exodus 33:22

Did Holy Spirit speak to you?

What would you add to the prayer to make it personal to you?

Day 13 - You Gave our Life

Good Morning Holy Spirit!

We are thankful this day. You loved us so much that you gave your life.

Although you finished your work on the Cross, we are perpetual recipients of what Your Love, Your Shed Blood, and Your Word provides.

You gave Life, Liberty, Love, Peace, Patience, Joy, Wisdom, Knowledge, Understanding, Discernment, Intercession, Forgiveness, Reconciliation, Healing, Miracles, Counsel, Might, Protection, Provision, and Strength, Comfort, a way of escape and a way to remain in right standing with you.

You gave us Abilities, Gifts, Fruit, Power, Signs, and Wonders.

You gave us a language with a direct line to you. Through this direct line, you communicate with us answers, strategies, plans, and instructions.

God, you are The Creator, Maker, and Ruler of all things. THE GREAT I AM. You gave us a destiny, a future, and a hope. You have given us a VICTORIOUS LIFE...Selah!

OUR PRAYER!

Day 13

Gentle Whispers from Holy Spirit

Today's Scriptures: John 3:16

Did Holy Spirit speak to you?

What would you add to the prayer to make it personal to you?

Day 14 - I Need Thee

Good Morning Holy Spirit!

As the Psalmist so eloquently sang, I need Thee, Oh I need Thee Every hour I need Thee, bless me now My Savior, I come, I come to Thee! (Robert Lowery-composer, Annie S.
Hawks- lyrics)

Lord, we are thankful that we serve a True and Living God. We need and desire to be in Your Presence.

You never sleep nor slumber. You are always available. You are never late, and you are always on time. There is no God like You.

You blessed us with life today. You blessed us with a song in our hearts today. You have already blessed us with provision and provided protection for us today.

You have blessed us with your unfailing and everlasting Love. We are blessed to know you as our God.

We are blessed to have a Relationship with a God like You.
No one can compare to how great and Wonderful you are...Selah!

We need Thee, OH we need Thee. Every hour we need Thee. Bless us now Our Savior. We come, we come to Thee!

OUR PRAYER!

Day 14

Gentle Whispers from Holy Spirit

Today's Scriptures: Jeremiah 10:10, 31:3; John 15:4-5; Psalms 18:30; 121:4; 143:1; Philippians 4:19

Did Holy Spirit speak to you?

What would you add to the prayer to make it personal to you?

Day 15 - Almighty to Perfection

Good Morning Holy Spirit!

LORD, oh LORD how MAJESTIC is YOUR NAME in ALL the earth.

You display Your SPLENDOR above the heavens and Your WILL in the earth.

If we searched the whole world over, only you LORD are ALMIGHTY TO PERFECTION!

There is nobody like You Lord. YOU ARE SOVEREIGN, RIGHTEOUS, and HOLY.

EXCELLENT is YOUR NAME!

There is nobody and no other god like You Lord!

OUR PRAYER!

Day 15

Gentle Whispers from Holy Spirit

Today's Scriptures: Psalms 8:1; Job 11:7; Matthew 6:10; and Jeremiah 10:6

Did Holy Spirit speak to you?

What would you add to the prayer to make it personal to you?

Day 16 - Right Relationship with You

Good Morning Holy Spirit!

You have made us More Than Conquerors through Christ, who loves us.

There is no greater victory we can have than being in Right Relationship with You. We are eternally grateful that no power, future or present, can separate us from Your Love.

The love revealed through CHRIST JESUS, the CROSS, and the GIFT of PROMISE. This is the TRUTH, and the HOLY SPIRIT of GOD CONFIRMS it!

OUR PRAYER!

Day 16

Gentle Whispers from Holy Spirit

Today's Scriptures: Romans 8:37-39; Acts 2:38; John 14:16; Acts 1:4

Did Holy Spirit speak to you?

What would you add to the prayer to make it personal to you?

Day 17 - Let Your Glory Reign

Good Morning Holy Spirit!

Thank you for opening everlasting doors and ancient gates. Throw open the floodgates of Heaven and pour out Your Blessings.

Let Your Blessings overtake us and Your GLORY Reign.

Fill Your House, let the heavens declare Your Righteousness, and Your Habitation.

Give thanks to the Lord, call upon His Name, and tell the nation's what He has done.

Let them know we serve a MIGHTY GOD! THE KING OF GLORY...Lift your head and LET HIM COME IN.

HE IS THE KING OF GLORY!

OUR PRAYER!

Day 17

Gentle Whispers from Holy Spirit

Today's Scriptures: Psalms 24:7, 10-9; 97:6; 26:8; 105:1; Malachi 3:10; Isaiah 12:4; Deuteronomy 28:2

Did Holy Spirit speak to you?

What would you add to the prayer to make it personal to you?

Day 18 - No God like Our God

Good Morning Holy Spirit!

Your Name is great and greatly to be praised.

Your Love is unfailing, Your Miracles are Mighty, and Your Wisdom is unmatched.

There is nothing too hard for you. Everything happens just as you say.

Thank You for allowing us to witness Your Great Promises, Great Creations, and Your Glorious Presence in our lives.

There is no God like our God!

OUR PRAYER!

Day 18

Gentle Whispers from Holy Spirit

Today's Scriptures: Psalms 96:4; Jeremiah 10:6; 32:17-25; Genesis 18:14; Mark 10:27; Luke 1:37

Did Holy Spirit speak to you?

What would you add to the prayer to make it personal to you?

Day 19 - Hearts for Worship

Good Morning Holy Spirit!

Thank You for giving us one heart and one purpose, to worship you forever.

You put a desire in our hearts for worship. And we choose to Worship You, King of kings and Lord of all lords.

No rocks can cry louder. No birds can chirp sweeter. Nothing can outdo the pursuit and passion we have to please and worship you.

We will sing and make melodies unto our God. We will make the sacrifice to Praise our Lord, God, and King.

Your Covenant is Everlasting, and your Promises never stop. Your Goodness for us is Eternal. For this brings You Great Joy.

Your Excellence has been signed, sealed, and witnessed by the Cross of Jesus.

OUR PRAYER!

Day 19

Gentle Whispers from Holy Spirit

Today's Scriptures: Jeremiah 10:10, 31:3; John 15:4-5; Psalms 18:30; 121:4; 143:1; Philippians 4:19

Did Holy Spirit speak to you?

What would you add to the prayer to make it personal to you?

Day 20 - Spiritual Helps

Good Morning Holy Spirit!

Thank You for giving us standing and staying power today!

You have given us Your Whole Armor (Spiritual Helps), to overcome temptations of the enemy. The Shield of Faith, Sword of the Spirit (the Word of God), a Lance (which is a pole weapon with spear carried by warriors), the Helmet of Salvation, Your Breastplate of Righteousness, a Belt of truth, Greaves (protection of the legs-knees to the ankles), and feet fitted with readiness given by the gospel of peace.

If the battle is ours, you have equipped us to take the spoils. We will not be tossed to and fro, scattered, and carried by the wind. We have been fixed and established to stand in faith (for Righteousness sake). And to Bring Glory to Your Name.

If the battle is yours, we will rest in you. We shall stand and see the Salvation of the Lord.

We shall see the Goodness of the Lord in the Land of the living, realizing that every battle is not ours to fight.

Thank You for Goodness and Mercy following us and for Your Righteous Right Hand.

Our confidence is in You!

OUR PRAYER!

Day 20

Gentle Whispers from Holy Spirit

Today's Scriptures: Ephesians 6:11-15; 2 Chronicles 20:15; Psalms 37:7; 62:5; 23:6; 27:13; Numbers 31:27

Did Holy Spirit speak to you?

What would you add to the prayer to make it personal to you?

Day 21 - The Lord of Our Salvation

Good Morning Holy Spirit!

"Great is Thy faithfulness! Great is Thy faithfulness! Morning by morning new mercies I see." All I have needed Thy hand hath provided, great is Thy faithfulness, Lord, unto me!" (Thomas Obadiah Chisholm)

Thank You for Your Faithful love. Love that never ends. Thank You for Mercies we sing of, mercies that never end.

You are the Lord of our inheritance; our hope and faith are in you. You are good to those who search for you. No god can compare.

We draw near to you and Praise Your Name.
Our confidence in you brings Great Recompense of
Reward. Our Souls depend and wait quietly. In
Your Word, we Hope.

For you are the Lord of our Salvation,
JEHOVAH M'KADDESH... God who sanctifies and
sets us apart.

OUR PRAYER!

Day 21

Gentle Whispers from Holy Spirit

**Today's Scriptures: Lamentation 3:22-26;
Psalms 52:9; 73:28; 103:5; Hebrews 10:35**

Did Holy Spirit speak to you?

What would you add to the prayer to make it
personal to you?

Day 22 - What We Have Is Greater

Good Morning Holy Spirit!

Thank You for Integrity and Truth. The Truth of Your Word.

We will not be trapped by the snare of the enemy or swayed by the words of others. For their words are as smooth as butter and more soothing than oil, but their swords are drawn, and their hearts are at war.

What we have is Greater. We are armored up today with our Spiritual Helps. The Whole Armor of God and crowned with the Mind of Christ.

We speak the truth which is The Word of God. We have the Sword of the Spirit and the Shield of Faith.

Thank You for honoring Your Word. We know that it shall not return void because you are attentive to Your Word. Your Promises are backed by ALL the HONOR of Your Name and Your Word.

When we pray you answer, encourage, and strengthen. You always hear Your Word and you answer.

Thank You for Your Heavenly Host of Angels. You are The Lord of Heaven's ARMY. The Lord of Host. We give You Praise.

OUR PRAYER!

Day 22

Gentle Whispers from Holy Spirit

Today's Scriptures: Matthew 22:16; Psalms 46:6; 55:21; 138:2-3; John 11:42; Ephesians 6: 10-18

Did Holy Spirit speak to you?

What would you add to the prayer to make it personal to you?

Day 23 - He Is Speaking

Good Morning Holy Spirit!

Thank You for showing us where to go and what to do.

Give us your plans and strategies, hold nothing back.

Tell us your secrets. The hidden things at the appointed times. Let us not be caught unaware or ignorant of the things of God! We will not be proud and refuse Your Word. The Word of the Lord.

Give us your wisdom, knowledge, and understanding.

Build us up and plant us in the right places. Make it a strong foundation. Set our faces like a stone determined to do your will.

What you tell us to do we will listen and obey.
Tune our Spirits to the Word of the Lord...He is
Speaking.

The Truth of Your Word is what you speak.

We love you, and we Trust You. Wisdom is crying
out loud in the street. Catch it...Selah!

OUR PRAYER!

Day 23

Gentle Whispers from Holy Spirit

Today's Scriptures: Jeremiah 29:11; 33:3; 42:1-22; 43:2; 2Timothy 3:16; John 15:15; Proverbs 1:20; 2:6; 1 Corinthians 2:10; 2 Corinthians 2:11

Did Holy Spirit speak to you?

What would you add to the prayer to make it personal to you?

Day 24 - The Lord, Our Shepherd

Good Morning Holy Spirit!

You are JEHOVAH-Rohi, The Lord, and our Shepherd. We shall not be in want. You feed us bread daily, fresh Manna from Heaven. You lead us to green pastures, yielding seed and producing good fruit.

You have provided Living Water, still water, a place of peace and rest. Not muddy and foul waters, but Purifying and Cleansing water. Water that will never run dry. You heal the brokenhearted, strengthen the weak, and set the captive free. You separate the sheep from the goats, and wheat from the tare. You are our protector. Our God of Justice. No fear shall be upon us except the fear of The Almighty God. Thank you for sending the Prince of Peace our Bright and Morning Star, Jesus.

Thank You for Your overflowing cup.

Anointed with the oil of joy. Smear it upon our heads, our minds, our thoughts, our imaginations, our souls, our hearts and our bodies. Overshadow us with Your Sweet Presence.

Thank You for Your Love, Your Goodness, and Your Mercy. They shall pursue us all the days of our lives.

We shall be your people Beholding Your Beauty and You shall be our God. Our Shepherd. JEHOVAH-ROHI.

OUR PRAYER!

Day 24

Gentle Whispers from Holy Spirit

Today's Scriptures: Jeremiah 10:10, 31:3; John
15:4-5; Psalms 18:30; 121:4; 143:1; Philippians
4:19

Did Holy Spirit speak to you?

What would you add to the prayer to make it
personal to you?

Day 25 - Covenant of Peace

Good Morning Holy Spirit!

You are JEHOVAH-SHALOM. Our God and Covenant of Peace. You allowed us to sleep in safety. You gave us sweet peace and sweet rest. You blessed our homes and family. You drive away danger from our lives. You protect us from danger seen and unseen.

You are for us, so who can stand against us? No weapon formed against us shall prosper and every tongue that rises against us, you shall condemn. Our righteousness is of you. Shower us with Your Blessings. Break the chains of bondage. Loose the shackles and fetters.

Thank you for rescuing us from the plots, plans, and schemes of the enemy. Thank you for security and safety that is found in you. The Secret Place of the HIGHEST GOD!

We are your People, the sheep of your pasture. You are our SOVEREIGN GOD!

OUR PRAYER!

Day 25

Gentle Whispers from Holy Spirit

Today's Scriptures: Ezekiel 34:25-31; Psalms 91, 121:8; Proverbs 3:24; Romans 8:31; Isaiah 54:17

Did Holy Spirit speak to you?

What would you add to the prayer to make it personal to you?

Day 26 - You Cleanse from Inside Out

Good Morning Holy Spirit!

Thank You for the greatest Miracle!
SALVATION!

Thank You for Your Cleansing Power. Your
Living, and Purifying Water. You cleanse from the
inside out.

Thank You for a new heart and a new Spirit. You
said, "Here I AM!" And you stood at the door and
knocked. We heard Your Voice, and we opened
the door to The Way, The Truth and New Life.

The way of passage to the Father, recognizing that
it was not a stranger's voice, but the voice of our
Creator,

The ALMIGHTY- GOD- EL SHADDAI! THE ALL SUFFICIENT GOD!
JEHOVAH! The Eternal and Everlasting One, I AM THAT I AM, THE ONE WHO IS AND WILL CONTINUE TO BE.

You took away the stony and stubborn heart, and you gave us a tender and responsive heart. A heart to seek after you...Your Voice and Your Love. We will be your people, and you will eternally be our God, I AM Selah!

OUR PRAYER!

Day 26

Gentle Whispers from Holy Spirit

Today's Scriptures: Ezekiel 36:22-38; Revelations 3:20; Genesis 21:33; 49:25; Jeremiah 32:27; John 10:5, 9-10; 14:6

Did Holy Spirit speak to you?

What would you add to the prayer to make it personal to you?

Day 27 - Save Lives, Save Souls, and Save Ourselves

Good Morning Holy Spirit!

Thank You for Your chosen watchman. Those who stand on the watchtower, stand on the wall, sit at the city gate, or walk through the valley.

Every position and location are important. Every position has a specific assignment. Thank you for equipping us and preparing us to do your will. Your God ordained assignment.

Help us to see the enemy coming and sound the alarm to save lives, save souls, and save ourselves.

Help us to continue to hear and deliver the Word of the Lord. Allow the Word to sink deep into our hearts and then deliver it to your people, never ashamed to Testify of Your Goodness.

Thank You for sensitivity to hear and see your movement and move with you. One heart, one mind, and one Spirit.

Thank you for a mind and will to follow your decrees and obey your regulations, for you are concerned about Your Holy Name and the representation of Your Holy Name. Your eyes roam to and fro looking to show yourself strong on behalf those whose heart is perfect towards you and Reveals Holiness before Your eyes. Your NAME is THE NAME among all NAMES. You are WORTHY OF ALL THE PRAISE and HONOR!

OUR PRAYER!

Day 27

Gentle Whispers from Holy Spirit

Today's Scriptures: Ezekiel 3:10; 33:1-9; 36:22-23; 37:1; Isaiah 21:8; Habakkuk 2:1; Proverbs 8:34; Hebrews 13:21; 2 Chronicles 16:9

Did Holy Spirit speak to you?

What would you add to the prayer to make it personal to you?

Day 28 - The Rock of Our Salvation

Good Morning Holy Spirit!

Your rule is everlasting, and Your Kingdom is Eternal. You are King of all kings and Lord of all lords. You rule over all the kingdoms of this world, and you give them to anyone you choose.

You exalt the humble and make low the proud. No one can compare to you in the heavens, on earth, or under the earth. You are Lord, and beside you, there is no other.

You declare, save, and proclaim Your Blessings upon Your people. You are the Rock of our Salvation. All Your acts are just and true. All honor and Glory belongs to you.

We Praise, Worship, and Honor our God who lives and reigns forever. JEHOVAH-ADONAI, our SOVEREIGN RULER. You have DIVINE DOMINION, and we surrender to you.

You are our MIGHTY GOD, SAVIOR AND KING!

OUR PRAYER!

Day 28

Gentle Whispers from Holy Spirit

Today's Scriptures: Daniel 4:31-37; Isaiah 43:11-12; 45:5; Psalms 3:8, 18:2; Philippians 2:10-11

Did Holy Spirit speak to you?

What would you add to the prayer to make it personal to you?

Day 29 - The Holy of Holies

Good Morning Holy Spirit!

Thank You Lord for the ability to approach you in the Secret Place.

As we move from the outer court, (the courtyard), to the inner court (the Sanctuary of the Temple), to Your Most Holy Place (the Inner room). The Holy of Holies.

Anoint us to minister to you, with clean hands and a pure heart; we bow before you. We offer ourselves to you and become the sacrifice of praise. We Proclaim allegiance to Your Name. We want Your Glory, the Glory of the Lord to appear and be revealed.

We want to hear the sound of your coming. The roar of rushing waters. We want to see the shine of Your Glory. The BRILLIANCE of Your Beauty and SPLENDOR.

Come in Lord, and rest your feet.
In The place of ABSOLUTE HOLINESS!

OUR PRAYER!

Day 29

Gentle Whispers from Holy Spirit

Today's Scriptures: Ezekiel 40:47-41:1-5; 43:1-12; Psalms 91:1; 24:4; Hebrews 13:15

Did Holy Spirit speak to you?

What would you add to the prayer to make it personal to you?

Day 30 - Our Desire is to Minister to You

Good Morning Holy Spirit!

At Your Presence, we will take careful notice of every instruction, every procedure, and every covenant. Using our Spiritual eyes and Spiritual ears. Attentive to You.

Lord, we surrender this time to you. Nothing is more important than being in Your Presence. We never want the consequences of being unfaithful to you.

We desire to bow in Your Presence, Minister to You, offer up a sacrifice of praise, and serve at Your Table, for you are our SOVEREIGN LORD.

OUR PRAYER!

Day 30

Gentle Whispers from Holy Spirit

Today's Scriptures: Ezekiel 44:1-31

Did Holy Spirit speak to you?

What would you add to the prayer to make it personal to you?

Day 31 - We Are Depending and Trusting in You

Good Morning Holy Spirit!

Fill us with Your Holy Presence. Your flowing water.

Make it a steady stream, never ceasing. Let our cups overflow. Lead us to the Healing River, a deeper place in you, where we can only swim in Your Presence. You must lead us there. We are depending, and trusting in you. It won't be ankle, knee, or waist deep.

It's an atmosphere, a space, a place, a moment in time of total surrender to you.

Your River flows through the desert and valley of the Dead Sea. Every dry place will spring forth, low places shall be made high, and every dead thing shall be resurrected. LIFE BE...LIFE COME FORTH!

Take us places we've never been. To things we have never seen, nor heard.

In Your River, it's too deep to walk along. Our faith and trust are in you. Higher heights and deeper depths are where we want to go in you. The LIVING WATERS and STREAMS. The Place of prosperity, peace, purification, life, liberty, love, and fruitfulness.

The water from Your Temple is always the right temperature, and it will never run dry. Fruit is abundant all year long for food and leaves for healing at YOUR RIVER.

OUR PRAYER!

Day 31

Gentle Whispers from Holy Spirit

Today's Scriptures: Ezekiel 47:1-12; Psalms 23:5; 42:7; 130:1; 1 Thessalonians 5:17; 1 Corinthians 2:9; Ephesians 3:18; Isaiah 45:2; John 11:43; Genesis 1:27

Did Holy Spirit speak to you?

What would you add to the prayer to make it personal to you?

Day 32 - Matters of Our Hearts, Conditions of Our Souls

Good Morning Holy Spirit!

You know the matters of our hearts and minds
today. Give us Your Wisdom,
Knowledge, Understanding, and Counsel.
Speak to us on how to deal with life, matters of
our hearts and conditions of our souls.

Peel through the layers of hardened hearts and
go to the core. The source of un-success and
failure. Touch the areas that need to be
touched. Heal and deliver the places that need
to be healed and delivered. Penetrate the
places where guilt, shame, hurt, pain, sickness,
and disease flourish. The place where only
bottles of tears can speak. The Secret matters
of the heart, Lord You know.

We seek counsel from our friend. Your Word says, the friendship of the Lord is for those that fear Him. You are our reliable friend that sticks closer than any brother. A friend that will never leave us nor forsake us.

A friend that gave His life for us and shed His Blood. A friend that forgives our sins and remembers them no more. A friend that never gives up on us.

He never blocks calls, refuses to answer the door, or gives inaccurate information.
He is HONORABLE and TRUE.

A friend with a righteous right hand.
He cleanses, purifies, and sanctifies the soul.
A true friend indeed, one that leads to the TRUTH OF HIS WORD.

SPEAK FRIEND; WE ARE LISTENING!

OUR PRAYER!

Day 32

Gentle Whispers from Holy Spirit

Today's Scriptures: 1 Corinthians 2:17; Job
15:8; 33:31; Psalms 25:14 (NHEB); 56:9;
Proverbs 18:24; Deuteronomy 31:7; 1 Timothy
2:6; Hebrews 8:12; Isaiah 41:10

Did Holy Spirit speak to you?

What would you add to the prayer to make it
personal to you?

Day 33 - Faithful and True

Good Morning Holy Spirit!

Thank You for helping us to be found faithful, responsible, and completely trustworthy in what you have called us to do.
When the enemy comes in like a flood and tries to use others to find fault, criticize, or condemn us, nothing will be found. When the laws change, distractions come, and life happens, we can stay the course.

Help us to continue to do what we have always done. Pray, Praise, Worship and stand on Your Word. Trusting and believing that you are for us. Therefore, who can be against us?

It is You God who causes those who are unsympathetic toward us, become deeply troubled, and change their standing decisions. It is You God who will cause those who were against us fast and ask God to intervene on our behalf.

The weapon may be formed against us, but it shall not prosper because the Greater lives inside of us. He will make our enemy our footstool.

Thank You for sending your angels to work on our behalf, to shut the mouths of the naysayers, and find us innocent in their sight. Many are the test and trials of the righteous, but You Shall, deliver us out of them all.

Thank You for restoration and order in our lives. Thank you for the assurance of knowing, when test and trials come, we know that our confidence and strength come from you. You never weaver. You are Faithful and True.

OUR PRAYER!

Day 33

Gentle Whispers from Holy Spirit

Today's Scriptures: Daniel 6:1-28; Isaiah 59:19; Romans 8:31; Isaiah 54:17; 1 John 4:4; Luke 20:43; Psalms 34:19; James 1:3

Did Holy Spirit speak to you?

What would you add to the prayer to make it personal to you?

Day 34 - No Relationship without Fellowship

Good Morning Holy Spirit!

Thank You for Brothers and Sisters that walk together in unity and oneness. Let the brotherly love continue as we walk in agreement. Equally yoked. For there is no relationship without fellowship. Like-minded in faith, having the same love. Unified with purpose and having a common goal.

There is nothing like lifting our voices together to our God and Praising His Holy Name! Blow the trumpet and clash the symbols with Praise and Thanksgiving. Sing to Lord. He is Good, His Love is faithful and endures forever!

OUR PRAYER!

Day 34

Gentle Whispers from Holy Spirit

Today's Scriptures: Amos 3:3; Ezra 3:8-13; Philippians 2:2-5

Did Holy Spirit speak to you?

What would you add to the prayer to make it personal to you?

Day 35 - Rise and Receive

Good Morning Holy Spirit!

Thank You for being with us and stirring up the gift within. We will not be fearful, anxious, and looking around in doubt, for you shall uphold us with Your Righteous Right Hand.

When we walk through the water, it shall not overflow. When we walk through the fire, we shall not smell like smoke. We shall take up our positions and stand strong for you shall bring deliverance.

The wise and righteous shall shine brightly as the stars and the sky, forever. Rise and receive the inheritance set aside for you! "I AM WITH YOU SAYS THE LORD!" THE LORD OF HEAVENS ARMIES has spoken!

OUR PRAYER!

Day 35

Gentle Whispers from Holy Spirit

Today's Scriptures: Daniel 12:3, 13; Haggar 1:13-15; Isaiah 41:10, 43:2, 2 Chronicles 20:17

Did Holy Spirit speak to you?

What would you add to the prayer to make it personal to you?

Day 36 - Your Eyes Are Searching

Good Morning Holy Spirit!

Thank You for Your Spirit that abides and remains in us. You're Temple. Your love Father is passionate and strong towards us and Your GLORY shall always surround us, in your presence.

Your eyes search the earth looking to and fro, and your oil pours out upon us from your olive branches and golden tubes.

It's by Your Spirit that nothing shall stand in our way.
You will make the way plain for us. The rough roads smooth and the crooked places straight. No mountain shall stand in our way. What we start we shall finish for we have been chosen and sent by you. You have placed your signet ring on our finger.

You will overthrow chariots and riders on our behalf.

Others will see and attest to Your Goodness towards us and Honor us when the assignment is complete, the foundation has been laid, and the last stone is set in place.

We will not despise small beginnings but rejoice because He who has begun a good work in us will continue His work until it is finished and complete.

We are confident not in our power and our might but the Spirit of the Lord of Host. The Lord of Heaven's ARMY!

OUR PRAYER!

Day 36

Gentle Whispers from Holy Spirit

Today's Scriptures: Haggai 2:20-22; Zechariah 1:14; 4:1-14; Isaiah 45:21; Philippians 1:6

Did Holy Spirit speak to you?

What would you add to the prayer to make it personal to you?

Day 37 - Agape Love

Good Morning Holy Spirit!

Thank You for Your consuming love and passion for us.

Your Agape Love! Love with no conditions, restrictions, and wrong motives attached. Just, pure, and genuine Love!

Thank You for families that sit together, walk together, play together, talk, communicate, and fellowship together, collectively. In our cities and towns, having and living peaceful lives.

Thank You, Father, for Your Provision, Protection, and for safety from all evil. Cover us with Your Blood!

Thank You for productive and hiring companies, job security, job safety, special projects, temporary assignments, promotional opportunities, educational advancement, benefits, and the fulfillment of needs, emotionally, mentally and physically.

Thank You for a Hope and a great future, generational inheritances, Seeds of peace and prosperity, sources of blessings, fruitful seasons, times of joy, rejoicing, and celebration.

We pray that people will receive and witness the Goodness of the Lord in the Land of the living through the lives of His Chosen people, Loving truth and peace as we celebrate Life Together!

OUR PRAYER!

Day 37

Gentle Whispers from Holy Spirit

**Today's Scriptures: Zechariah 8:1-23;
Jeremiah 29:11; Psalms 27:13; 1 Corinthians
13:4**

Did Holy Spirit speak to you?

What would you add to the prayer to make it
personal to you?

Day 38 - Refresh, Restore, and Renew

Good Morning Holy Spirit!

Send Your Rain. Saturate the dry lands and make lush your fields. Strengthen, Restore, and Comfort.

Receive the broken-hearted, wounded, and rejected.

Wash away the ungodly thoughts and memories, and fill us with Your Joy and Love.

Refresh, Restore, and Renew. Make us glorious, white as snow, and refined as silver and gold.

Cleanse our hands and purify our hearts. Redeem Your Precious Jewels. By Your Power make us strong. With you, we are victorious.

With you, we are mighty and tall.

OUR PRAYER!

Day 38

Gentle Whispers from Holy Spirit

Today's Scriptures: Zechariah 10:1-10; 13:9;
Psalms 24:4; 57:1

Did Holy Spirit speak to you?

What would you add to the prayer to make it personal to you?

Day 39 - Captivity

Good Morning Holy Spirit!

Father, we know that negative thoughts and feelings of disrespect and dishonor, if not taken captive, will often lead to spirits of rage, manipulation, and control. If they linger for extended periods of time, eventually they will lead to plots and plans for murder, be it physically or mentally.

This spirit will lead some people and people groups, even nations into spirits of confusion, torment, anxiety, stress, heart issues, fear of death, and eventually death.

Father, we know that this is not your plan. Salvation has always been your ultimate plan. Love and unity have always been your plan because you love us, and you gave Your Only Son so that we could live and have eternal life.

We thank you for your plan and for those who will stand for our nation. We thank you for those who will Fast, Pray, and Intercede for Righteousness, unity, and justice, "For such a time as this."

You are King of all kings and Lord of all lords. We must come to you for strategies and righteous plans to combat the enemy and restore peace. We seek Your Wisdom today. Teach us, show us, prepare us, and equip us.

OUR PRAYER!

Day 39

Gentle Whispers from Holy Spirit

Today's Scriptures: Esther 1-4:17; John 3:16; 2 Corinthians 10:5

Did Holy Spirit speak to you?

What would you add to the prayer to make it personal to you?

Day 40 - Sweet Fragrance

Good Morning Holy Spirit!

Help us to set our minds on things above, eternal, unseen, and worthy of Your Praise. Things that are true, honorable, right, pure, and lovely, of good report and great Excellency. Things that will cause us to triumph in Christ Jesus.

May these things ascend to heaven as a sweet-smelling aroma, blazing fire of sacrificial praise, and a pleasing fragrance to your nostrils?

As we think and live out these things, help us to spread the fragrance, knowledge, and love of you. For Your Name alone is like purified oil and soothing ointment to our souls.

Thank You for the fragrance of your sacrificial offering.

You laid down Your Life to be a sweet-smelling savor to our God and an unspeakable gift for us!

You are The Rose of Sharon and the Lilly of the valley.

You are the Truth that sprung up from the earth when Loving Kindness and Truth met together, and Righteousness and Peace kissed each other.

We adore inhaling the bouquet and Glorious aroma of Your Presence. Saturate our Atmosphere today.

OUR PRAYER!

Day 40

Gentle Whispers from Holy Spirit

**Today's Scriptures: Psalms 85:10-11;
Ephesians 5:2; 2 Corinthians 4:18; 9:15;
Colossians 3:2; Philippians 4:8**

Did Holy Spirit speak to you?

What would you add to the prayer to make it personal to you?

Day 41 - Chosen by God

Good Morning Holy Spirit!

Thank you for people that speak life to our Souls.

Those that make our Spirits leap in their presence.

Those that fill our hearts with boundless Joy and Blessings. Spiritual Fathers and Mothers, brothers and sisters.

People of purpose. Chosen by God to speak Words of Wisdom and Knowledge from the Lord. Those that edify, exalt, and build up.

Thank You for the Chosen that are blessed because they trust God's Word and operate in the Gift and Spirit of Faith. Those that breathe out the fruit of Love.
Those that sing, cry, and rejoice with us and for us.
Those that stand for us and with us without wavering.

Surely the Hand of the Lord is upon them to be a Blessing to us in such a distinct way.

God Bless us all to be that Chosen person, for someone. That one who will share the gift of God's Love!

OUR PRAYER!

Day 41

Gentle Whispers from Holy Spirit

Today's Scriptures: Luke 1:26-45; Romans 12:6-8; 1 Thessalonians 5:11; 2 Corinthians 4:13; 1 Corinthians 12:8-10; 14:3

Did Holy Spirit speak to you?

What would you add to the prayer to make it personal to you?

Day 42 - A New Way of Loving and Living

Good Morning Holy Spirit!

Thank you for the rising sun sent from heaven and the fresh morning breeze. Thank You for the dawn of a new day. A manifestation of God from heaven.

Thank You for a new way of thinking - having the mind of Christ. A new way of loving - unconditionally. A new way of living - overshadowed by your prosperity and peace. A new way of caring - full of compassion, loving our neighbor as our selves.

Lead us Holy Spirit. If it's Your cloud by day, fire by night, eastern star in the heavens, a sign or wonder, a night dream, an open vision, a messenger sent by God or an angelic visitation. We are open and submitted to you and your ways.

Show us, teach us, tell us, somehow, and reveal to us your plans and strategies. We yield our bodies and souls to you and your rules of engagement.

Take us where you want us to go. Guide our feet into the path of peace. Fill us with Your Wisdom.

Bless us with Your Favor, good health, and Mighty Strength. Reveal your thoughts and plans. Prepare the way for us. Help us to demonstrate, by the way that we live, that we are Christians. Christ-like servants sent by God.

OUR PRAYER!

Day 42

Gentle Whispers from Holy Spirit

Today's Scriptures: Luke 1:78-80; 2:25-35; 39-52; Matthew 2:13; Exodus 13:21

Did Holy Spirit speak to you?

What would you add to the prayer to make it personal to you?

Day 43 - Cleanse Us

Good Morning Holy Spirit!

Baptize us with Your Sweet Spirit today. Forgive us of our sins. Sever any ungodly roots and soul ties. Separate the chaff from the wheat. Purge the toxic thoughts and negative memories from our hearts and minds.

Lose any toxic experiences the enemy may use against us, to keep us bound. Reveal to us any idol, thing, or individual in our lives that does not contribute to the production of good, healthy, and nourishing fruit.

Cleanse the threshing floor and discard/ remove anything that yields inadequate returns, profitless activities, or mindless resources. Throw them into the never-ending fire and cleanse our hearts and minds.

Free us so that we can walk in the Fruit of the Spirit and exercise our Spiritual Helps.

Fill our barns and storehouses with good fruit and people with Godly wisdom.

Go before us and prepare the way. Fill the valleys. Level the mountains and hills. Straighten the curves and smooth the rough places.

Help us to carry out the will of God and All that you require of us. For our desire is to please you and bring You Immense Joy!

OUR PRAYER!

Day 43

Gentle Whispers from Holy Spirit

Today's Scriptures: Luke 3; Matthew 3:13-17; Mark 1: 1-8

Did Holy Spirit speak to you?

What would you add to the prayer to make it personal to you?

Day 44 - Glory at Your Table

Good Morning Holy Spirit!

Help us to recognize Your Presence in our lives. During the pace of life, help us to identify you and acknowledge your existence.

When you walk through the crowd or through the wall. When you enter the Door or come our Way, help us to see the Splendor of Your Glory.

Help us to hear your still small voice, and feel Your Loving, Comforting, and Healing touch. Help us to smell the sweet Aroma of Heaven's thrown and taste and see how good you really are.

As we sit at your table today, help us recognize Your Presence. For it is at your table that we are graced to use all five of our senses. As we sit down and bless Your Holy Name today, we can be thankful because you woke us this morning. We have eyes to see, ears to hear, feeling in our limbs, noses to smell, and taste in our mouths.

We can be thankful because you continue to feed us with fresh Bread, Manna from heaven, morning by morning. You satisfy us with the Milk and Meat of Your Holy Word, Fruit of the Spirit, and the press of your anointed oil. You offer salt full of Your Savor, and you refresh us with cups Your Living Water, to overflowing and never-ending supply.

You are always on time and consistently satisfying. Help us to use our five senses to identify Your Presence in our lives.

Remind us of the simple pleasures of life. Things we sometimes take for granted.

Thank You for spreading the table and making provisions for us today.

OUR PRAYER!

Day 44

Gentle Whispers from Holy Spirit

Today's Scriptures: John 1:26; 4:13-14; 6:32; 10:9; 14:6; 20: 19-20; Luke 4:30; 14:34; Exodus 16:4; 1 Peter 2:2; 1 Corinthians 3:2; Galatians 5:22-23; Deuteronomy 8:7-8

Did Holy Spirit speak to you?

What would you add to the prayer to make it personal to you?

Day 45 - Mediator

Good Morning Holy Spirit!

Thank You for Revelation that comes from an Open
Heaven. Thank You, Jesus, for being the stairway
between Heaven and Earth. The mediator between
God and Man.
The Advocate.
The Christ.
The Door.
The Lamb.
The Life.
The True God.
The True Light.
The True Vine.
The Truth.
The Vine. The
Way, and the
Word.

OUR PRAYER!

Day 45

Gentle Whispers from Holy Spirit

Today's Scriptures: John 1:1, 9, 14, 29, 51; 8:12; 10:7,9; 11:25; 14:6; 15:1,5; 1 Timothy 2:5; 1 John 2:1, 5:20; Mark 14:61

Did Holy Spirit speak to you?

What would you add to the prayer to make it personal to you?

Day 46 - The Gift of the Promise

Good Morning Holy Spirit,

Thank you for a fresh bubbling spring that flows from within. The spring that gives eternal life and never runs dry.

Thank You for not discriminating. Anyone can drink from this well, if thirsty. Once you draw from it, you will never have to return. In fact, with this well, you don't need a bucket or a rope. You can leave your jar in the well because it is no longer needed. For the water will move from an external well and into an internal bubbling and flowing spring within.
It's an inside job with eternal benefits.

Thank you for the Spiritual Gift that was given by the Messiah, Jesus. The gift that will make others want to come and see a Heavenly Man named Jesus. The One who was sent by God, to save a dying world.

God, you are Spirit, and you are Truth. We are your worshipers. Thank You for sending Your Son to save us.

Thank You for the Gift of the Promise that was sent back to earth, just for us on the day of Pentecost.

Thank you for the freedom to pray, sing, and move by Your Spirit.

OUR PRAYER!

Day 46

Gentle Whispers from Holy Spirit

Today's Scriptures: John 4:1-38; Acts 2:1-13

Did Holy Spirit speak to you?

What would you add to the prayer to make it personal to you?

Day 47 - Your Spirit Anoints and Equips

Good Morning Holy Spirit!

Thank You for Your Spirit that anoints and equips us to proclaim the Good News. The Spirit that helps us represent you, by being fruitful and productive citizens, to unbelievers.

Help us to speak life to the captive so that burdens can be removed, yokes destroyed, and the oppressed be set free.

Help us to operate with a Spirit of Faith, Discernment, Healing, and Working of Miracles so that blinded eyes may be open, and all manner of sickness and disease be healed. Help us to bring light to dark places and life to dead places.

We are atmosphere changer and Glory carriers. We have been sent by God to break up the fallow ground, pluck up weeds, and thorns to bring forth righteous seed.

Thank You for a harvest of souls that are ripe and processed for eternal life. With God, all things are possible. There is nothing impossible for our God. He is Creator, Maker, and Ruler of All.

Thank You for grace and favor with God and with men.

OUR PRAYER!

Day 47

Gentle Whispers from Holy Spirit

**Today's Scriptures: Genesis 1:28; Proverbs
3:4; Jeremiah 4:3; Matthew 11:30, 19:26; Luke
1:37, 4:17-21; 1 Corinthians 12:8-10; Colossians
1:16**

Did Holy Spirit speak to you?

What would you add to the prayer to make it
personal to you?

Day 48 - The Shifting of Seasons, Times, and Directions

Good Morning Holy Spirit!

Thank You for helping us recognize times of transition.

According to Matthew 4:12-17, when Jesus learned that John the Baptist had been arrested and the prophecy of Isaiah had been fulfilled, He began to preach, "Repent of your sins and turn to God, for the Kingdom of Heaven is near."

Lord help us to recognize the shifting of your seasons, times, and directions. As we let go of the old, help us to take hold of the new thing you have in store for us, and embrace it.
We are thankful for the new transition and transformation that will bring about a manifestation and demonstration of your Power. It shall spring forth, and we shall see it. Others will witness the transition and acknowledge that it is of

the Lord. Help us to recognize your voice during this time of conversion.

It's a part of the metamorphosis; we shall not ignore the development of each phase in this process.

Help us to follow and obey you as You Guide us through the process. Help us to pick up the assignment that has been passed on to us with joy and exceeding gladness.

Thank You for advancements and Kingdom Promotions. We shall not be moved by naysayers, fear, or the offense of others. We shall remain steadfast and unmovable, pursuing our goals. The Heavenly Call. For there is a prize. We shall reap and not faint.

OUR PRAYER!

Day 48

Gentle Whispers from Holy Spirit

Today's Scriptures: Philippians 3:14; Matthew 5:12; Isaiah 43:19

Did Holy Spirit speak to you?

What would you add to the prayer to make it personal to you?

Day 49 - Loved Ones

Good Morning Holy Spirit!

Thank you for loved ones, spouses, and friends that will go to Jesus on Your behalf. Those who will bring you to Jesus and stand in His Presence with you.

Those that won't let any obstacle stand in their way.

They have faith in you that can be seen, heard, and demonstrated. They won't back down or take "no" for an answer. They will walk with you, talk for you, stand with you, fight for you, carry you, and Pray and Intercede for you when you are not strong enough or able to do it for yourself.

They are not people who try to demonstrate one thing, but in their hearts, think or feel another. There is a genuine Love for one another and a desire to see immense success.
This is a divine relationship ordained by God that others may not understand.

Thank you for spouses, friends, sisters, and brothers that love at all times. They will encourage, forgive, equip, edify, exalt and lift up.

No matter what the onlookers say, they won't back down because they love you with the love of the Lord.

OUR PRAYER!

Day 49

Gentle Whispers from Holy Spirit

Today's Scriptures: Mark 2:1-12; Matthew 9:1-8; Proverbs 17:17; Romans 12:9, 13:10, Mark 12:31; 1 Corinthians 13:4-8, 13; Ephesians 4:2; 1 Peter 4:8

Did Holy Spirit speak to you?

What would you add to the prayer to make it personal to you?

Day 50 - Secrets and Hidden Things

Good Morning Holy Spirit!

Thank you, Holy Spirit, for joining Jesus and remaining with Him as He demonstrated to us how to Pray a Prayer of Thanksgiving, and how to honor, appreciate, obey, and please The Father.

Jesus, you displayed outwardly your inward perception of Love toward the Father. And in return, you demonstrated your love for us by being a Godly example to us. You were determined to reveal Your Father to us and the Secrets of the Kingdom of God because you knew it pleased the Father.

Thank you for uncovering the hidden things. Thank You for doing all that God had entrusted you to do, including, enduring the Cross, and sending down the Holy Spirit of God after you ascended to heaven and took your seat at the right hand of the Father.

Thank you for making Intercession for us and finishing your assignment. Thank You for equipping us and giving us rest in exchange for our weariness and our heavy burdens. You make them easy and light. Teach us how to have humbled and gentle hearts.

Teach us how to trust in the Father's Love and be Thankful. For in all things, we are to give Thanks.

OUR PRAYER!

Day 50

Gentle Whispers from Holy Spirit

Today's Scriptures: Matthew 11:25-30; John 1:32, 19:30; Deuteronomy 29:29; 1 Corinthians 2:10; Ephesians 1:9-12; 1 Thessalonians 5:18; Acts 1:9-12

Did Holy Spirit speak to you?

What would you add to the prayer to make it personal to you?

Thank you for sharing 50 days of prayer with me.
I am honored and grateful that you allowed me to share
in your devotional time with God.
I pray that you have been richly blessed.

Dr. Troye

As HE SPEAKS...I write.

About the Author

Dr. Troye is a child of the Most High God, Wife, Mother, Educator, Minister, Chaplain, Intercessor, Author, Blogger, Student, and Founder of **The Prayer Tent International.**

She desires to pray the heart of God and to reach the masses, through various social media platforms, with Revelation and Knowledge of God's Word through Teaching and Prayer.

Dr. Troye is an active Blogger, she sends out Good Morning Holy Spirit and Thank You Holy Spirit Tweets. She is also committed to three o'clock, evening prayer. This is the time according to Acts 4:31, that the Disciples prayed, and the earth started shaking. They were filled with the Holy Spirit of God, began to speak boldly, and preach the Word of God. She calls it, "Earth Shaking Prayer!"

Dr. Troye has served in local ministries in the states of Alabama, Florida, Georgia, and now in Missouri where she currently resides.

Dr. Troye has served in ministry for over 20 years. She was licensed and ordained in 2014 through Word of Life Ministries International and Word of Life Christian Fellowship, as a Minister and Chaplain.

Her passion and desire is to see others whole, walking in their God-given Authority, full of God's Wisdom and fulfilling their God-given Purpose.

You may contact Dr. Troye at:

Website: theprayertentinternational.org

Email: DrTroye@theprayertentinternational.org

The Prayer Tent Int. @Twitter

The Prayer Tent International @Facebook

The Prayer Tent International.wordpress.com

This book is a series of interactive prayers/meditations that cause you to explore your relationship with Holy Spirit. Upon completion of this book, you will want to share it with family and friends because you will want them to experience Holy Spirit as you have.

Dr. Dominique Baptist, President
Spirit &Truth Christian University

Enjoy this devotional; it is a gift from God through Dr. Troye to be a blessing to you! Your spirit will be fed: thus bringing strength, encouragement, and wisdom to support you in dealing with the multiple battles that you face every day.

Apostle Roger C. Kelly Sr., CLU, ChFC
Eaglevision Consulting Group

Dr. Troye has eloquently and effectively composed and compiled a book of prayers that will serve as a resource, as well as a source to help direct you to "The Source." Remember, the way we communicate with our Creator is through prayer. Pray to jumpstart your day!

Anita Hawkins Nowlen
Certified Diversity Trainer/Life Coach
Women's Issues

Made in the USA
Lexington, KY
04 August 2019